ONE GOD, ONE RELIGION, ONE LIFE

ONE GOD, ONE RELIGION, ONE LIFE

Ahsan Ali Syed

PARTRIDGE

A Penguin Random House Company

Library of Congress Control Number: 2015941396
ISBN: Hardcover   978-1-4828-3139-9
               Softcover   978-1-4828-3138-2
               eBook   978-1-4828-3140-5

Print information available on the last page.

To order additional copies of this book, contact
Toll Free 800 101 2657 (Singapore)
Toll Free 1 800 81 7340 (Malaysia)
orders.singapore@partridgepublishing.com

www.partridgepublishing.com/singapore

Beyond human explanations, perceptions, imagination, comprehension is the truth of unity' (one God).

*Dedicated to my mentor, master and my guide **Sayedna Hussein, Son of Ali. Grandson of Abu Talib (Peace be upon them)**.*

PREFACE

In the Name of Allah to whom all the Glory Belongs and to Whom is our Return. This Book would not be possible without the blessings of my mentor, master and my guide Sayedna Hussein, Son of Ali, Son of Abu Talib **(Peace be upon them)** whose sacrifice cannot be forgotten. I will continue this work bestowed on me and will carry on to serve the Almighty and the pious household of Ahle Bait till the last breath of my life.

*Who wears this world; as a pair of glasses
to see his hereafter is intelligent.*

Use this world; only that much its usage is not a burden on you,
when you depart its separation doesn't Sadden you.

Extravagance in materialism leads to destruction,
Extravagance in spiritualism leads to rejuvenation.

To be privileged is mercy of God,
to share it with underprivileged is
acknowledgment of that mercy.

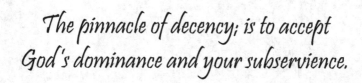

The pinnacle of decency; is to accept
God's dominance and your subservience.

Evolving your inner self, to meet with your Creator is a life spent with prudence.

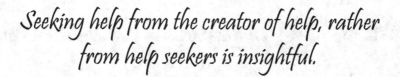

Seeking help from the creator of help, rather from help seekers is insightful.

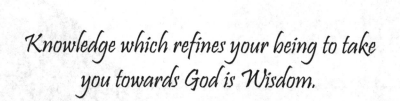

Knowledge which refines your being to take you towards God is Wisdom.

Astute is one who pass through this world for hereafter,
as a traveler, who pass through mirage in the desert.

Brilliance; is to understand behind every success is God's capabilities not his own.

Purity of faith; does not make you depend on dependable, but on unsurpassable (God).

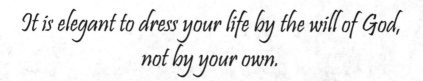

It is elegant to dress your life by the will of God, not by your own.

The best capitalism is to capitalize on the promise of sovereign God.

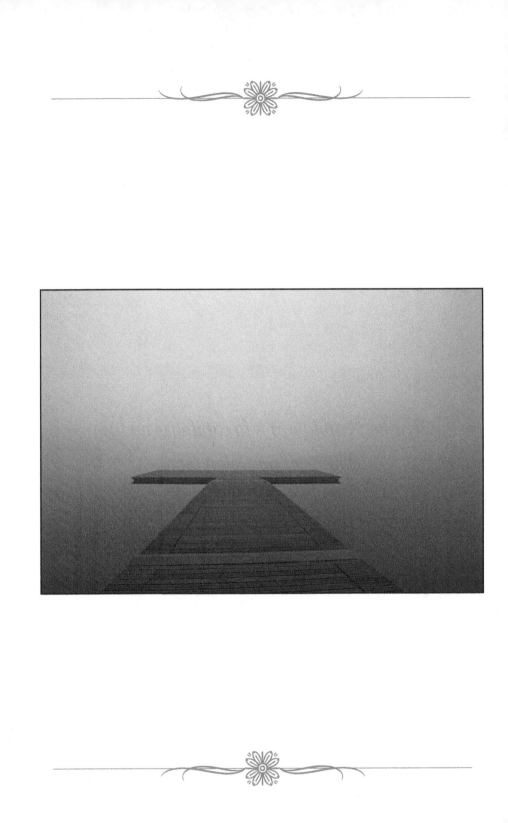

An expert investor is one, who barters his help
to the poor with God's help to him.

Self-restrictions on desires to limit his needs,
to protect others needs is virtuous.

One who is devout towards God,
often shelters an orphan,
in a like manner they shelter
their own child.

Infallible always understand there is logic of God behind every creation.
They always strive to protect such logic.

Charity; with zero disclosure to protect the identity of deserving is an act of compassionate man.

Nobility is the spirit of courage,
courageous- is the attitude of selfless,
selfless is to live and die for God.

One who removes humanity out of ignorance,
to guide them to eternal bliss through his ability
is precocious.

Earn with the intention to uplift the poor,
pray with the intention to uplift your soul.

Social reform comes through propagation of human freedom. Human freedom is the best way of propagating God.

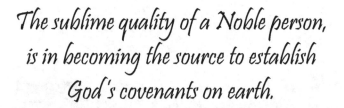

*The sublime quality of a Noble person,
is in becoming the source to establish
God's covenants on earth.*

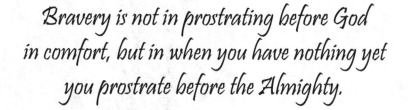

Bravery is not in prostrating before God
in comfort, but in when you have nothing yet
you prostrate before the Almighty.

To be spontaneous; is to answer God's call exactly at the prescribed times of the day.

Often actions done to gain human appreciations are recognised on earth, but wasted in the heaven.

Those who don't take cognisance of their
own acts, are often judgmental about others.

A contamination cautious cleanses his soul,
usually how a normal person cleanses his body.

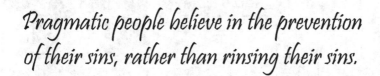

Pragmatic people believe in the prevention of their sins, rather than rinsing their sins.

The observer is watchful of his deeds
in this material world, to enhance his position
in the hereafter.

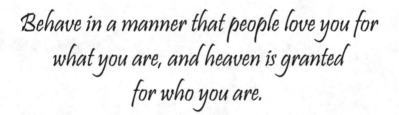

*Behave in a manner that people love you for
what you are, and heaven is granted
for who you are.*

Why is it difficult to understand
every morning,
one can wake up, then why one cannot wake up
after death by God's will.

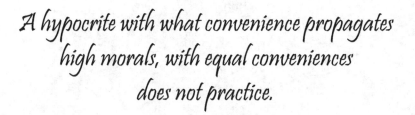

A hypocrite with what convenience propagates high morals, with equal conveniences does not practice.

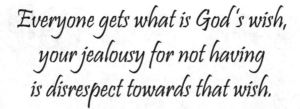

Everyone gets what is God's wish,
your jealousy for not having
is disrespect towards that wish.

It is wonderful to dream about heaven; what is more wonderful is to achieve your dream.

How sad after 1400 years we are still at educating to pray on time, when Prophet Muhammad (Peace be upon him) taught us, Allah is Omnipresent and needs to be remembered all the time.

To recognise the importance of your mother is an art of kind men, equally if not more, to recognise the importance of the mother of your child is an art of just men.

It is to live in fools paradise to commit sin in secrecy and imagine no one saw you, and however God was watching you.

To repeat the act of worship before unwarranted people
is the habit of a pompous man,
to repeat an act of worship secretly before God
is habit of a humble man.

How could you ever rest from thanking God,
when the ability to thank is also given by God.

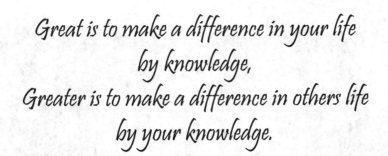

Great is to make a difference in your life
by knowledge,
Greater is to make a difference in others life
by your knowledge.

Why does one ponder on life and death so much, when both are not under his command.

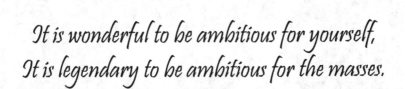

It is wonderful to be ambitious for yourself,
It is legendary to be ambitious for the masses.

Persistent consistency in humility
and submission; will help you
not to lose your God.

The most privileged communication,
is in a submission that allows you
to feel God's presence.

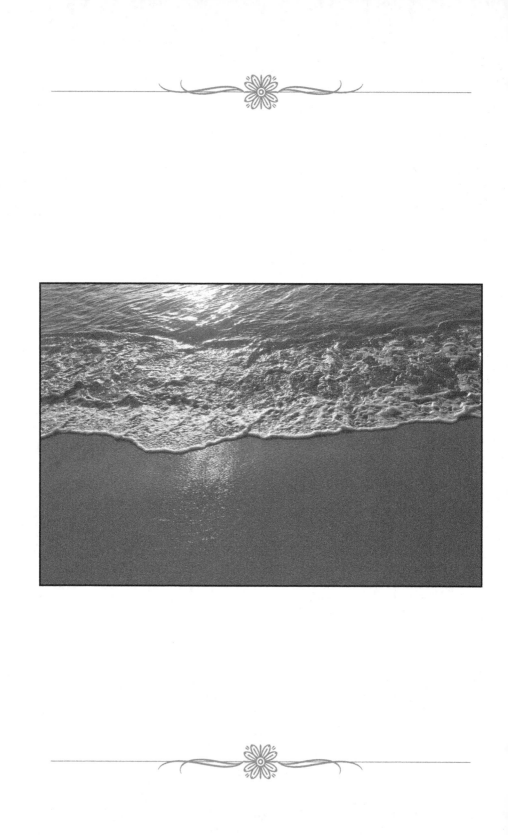

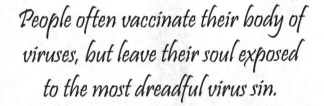

People often vaccinate their body of viruses, but leave their soul exposed to the most dreadful virus sin.

God is everywhere;
to visualize God all you need is
to have a pure heart
with a clear vision.

The way darkness enhances the beauty of the moon, similarly, trial enhances the beauty of faith.

The God I know is so generous that he gives believers or unbelievers without discrimination, why do you discriminate than.

The biggest triumph is
to win over your own desires.

Sagacious trains his tongue and actions with intellect, to make his acts a definition of immortality.

Control your tongue with your
pious mind and actions, with your
God-fearing heart to be notable.

Success, peace and tranquility come with planning, planning is the art of planners and God is the best of planners one can have.

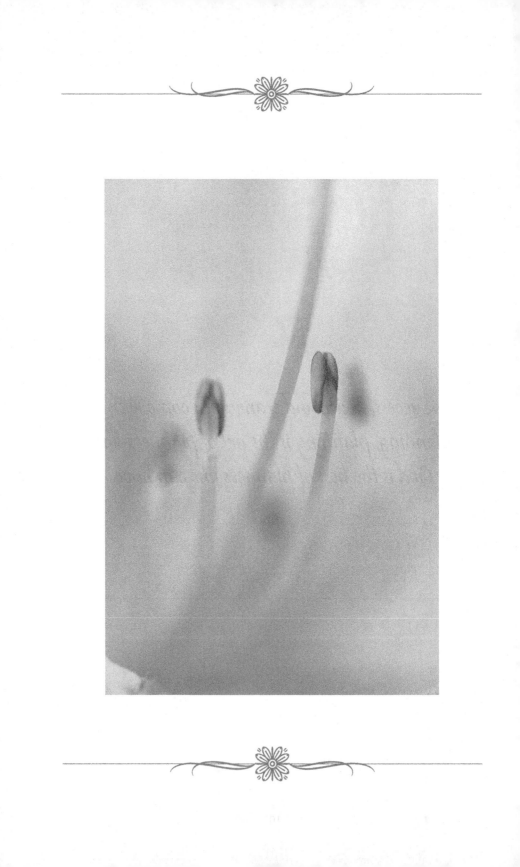

Faith in God, is the most valuable possession, its admiration is in the way it is practiced and protected.

Printed in the United States
By Bookmasters